Beautiful Astrology's
Venus Retrograde
GUIDE & WORKBOOK

a creative process for
clarity and insight

Melanie Gurley

EARTH
DRAGON
PRESS

Cover art by Leah Rose
Illustrations by Leah Rose and E. Edwards
Book design and layout by Ted Owen
Edited by Elizabeth Russell

Printed in the United States of America.

ISBN: 979-8-9870913-2-6

Earth Dragon Press
Eugene, Oregon
2023

Dedicated to the beauty that
Venus represents and to souls who
are called to explore their own
becoming in real time.

Acknowledgements

Contents

INTRODUCTION

"There is no solution to anything unless Venus is involved – unless beauty and love are present."

~Caroline Casey

Introduction

Welcome to Beautiful Astrology! Here we aim to engage with our personal astrology in real time, making meaning by recognizing patterns and contextualizing our experience.

To this end, I'm pleased to introduce a simple engagement process specifically for retrograde periods. Over several years of guiding clients in my planetary Retrograde Clubs, I developed and honed the "Retrograde Tracking Kit" to bring insight and discovery to these astrological cycles. That "kit" has grown into this, the first in a series of retrograde guides designed to support your astrological journey. In particular, I've witnessed my clients finding special support from the Magical Touchstone which is built into the Beautiful Astrology Process, about which you'll learn more about as we progress.

My focus on retrogrades stems from the fact that almost every reading I was doing for clients over several years centered around these times of not-knowing — varying in duration and depth — but still, revolving around various planetary retrograde periods. It was witnessing this repeated need for guidance during these times that led me to create Tracking Kits and Clubs in the first place. There was such a welcome response from the participants that I wanted to expand the reach of this process and make it more accessible by putting it into a self-guided format.

In the following pages, you will find the next iteration of this retrograde support structure, which includes a brief orientation to what we are working with and how to make it your own.

Aside from this introductory reading, there are three main parts to the book, beginning with Preparation, where you will be guided through the Beautiful Astrology Process that has been developed through the Retrograde Clubs. The Preparation section culminates in developing your own Magical Touchstone, a keyword-inspired phrase or other creation. This Magical Touchstone will be your ally during your journey. Then, we have the tracking pages of the Engagement section for you to log your experience, helping you stay aware of themes as they develop. Next, there is a short but important section for Reflection, where you'll sort out what you've gone through. In addition, you will find supportive resources in the Appendices at the back of the book.

The technical information and 'astrologese' has been kept intentionally sparse in order to make room for you to explore your experience in real time as it relates to the timing and themes of the retrograde cycle, without getting too bogged down with technicalities. Focusing on the quality and flavor of your experience and how it relates to the themes at hand — particularly your Magical Touchstone that you will create for this retrograde period — allows most people to deepen their relationship to what is happening, rather than becoming distracted with a bunch of heady material.

There are a few terms you'll want to be familiar with during your reading. Rather than listing them out in a glossary, they have been peppered throughout the text, showing up just when you need them. Head on over!

ORIENTATION

"Dwell on the
beauty of life."

~Marcus Aurelius

Orientation

One of the great benefits of seeing time through the lens of astrology is that we become familiar with the idea that time has undulating qualities that cycle past in a variety of speeds, durations, and magnitudes.

While a self-aware person may be able to track themes that come up in their life without the use of astrology, the benefit that is offered through pointed tracking gives anyone a leg up, not only in noticing such themes, but also in generating a broader perspective within which the themes are situated. This deepens personal meaning and contextualizes what might otherwise just be confusing or difficult to string together because of the way the various qualities move through time at different rates.

Astrological tracking gives us a helpful hand by lending the ability to anticipate when certain themes or qualities of time will be here, how long they may last, and in what parts of life they are likely to show up. It's really quite remarkable.

Though we do have this wonderful way of seeing that can help point us in the right direction or offer us an outline of what may come, it is important to approach this material from a grounded and centered place, while also maintaining space for magic and mystery to come through. We don't want to pretend we know exactly what may pass — nor talk ourselves into the worst possible outcome!

Keeping a space of trusting curiosity is the best approach. Practice staying in the moment. This creates a good basis to move from as you enter a timeline with potential challenges and unforeseen opportunities. And, if you find yourself overly stressed, perhaps finding a supportive friend, mentor, or therapist may be the right move for you. Please always take care of yourself and do what's right for you.

Now let's take some time to get acquainted with natal charts before we begin to use them in the next section, where we will learn what a retrograde is and how to find it in your chart.

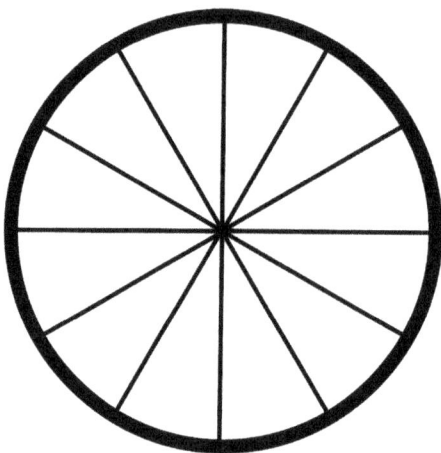

Natal Chart — a "snapshot" of the sky at the moment you were born, from the location you were born. It is a 2-D rendition of a 3-D reality, most often rendered in a circular diagram form. It can be thought of as a "fingerprint" of the quality of time at a particular moment, from a specific earthly location. It never changes, but is instead a constant — like your actual fingerprint! Your natal chart can be thought of to bear your "potentials", which are then released over time. So, in that sense, it is rather less static than most other fixed diagrams, and more dynamic than it may seem! It shows which sign each of the Planets was in at the moment of your birth.

Aside from the placements of the planets in signs, another important facet of the natal chart is Houses, which describe where in your life a particular energy is likely to show up.

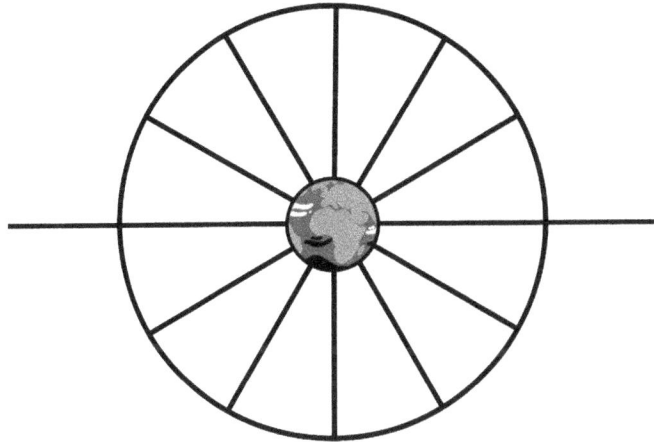

House — one of 12 "pie slices" of the sky which encircles us. The houses are anchored to the viewer's location here on the Earth (or to your location of birth in your natal chart). Rather than being anchored to any particular star, group of stars, or a particular span of the heavens, houses relate to the horizon at the moment of viewing, which is always changing as we rotate on our axis, day in and day out. There are 6 houses above the horizon, and 6 houses below. The houses signify different parts of our lives where the energies of signs and planets show up and play out. In our Natal Charts, they are static, just like the planets. In fact, they are always static. It is the sky which moves through these imaginary pie slices of the sky around us. You might think of them as 12 different windows, set in a circle, through which we view the heavens. Whatever part of the sky you see through your window is the "sign" that is in that "house".

Now we know what a Natal Chart is and what the pie slices called Houses are. You probably already have a sense of what the signs of the Zodiac are — or at least what they can mean. But, just in case you are new to either, I have defined them below, with the Zodiac coming first, because it is simpler.

Zodiac — a band of sky that encircles the Earth, conceptually broken into 12 equal parts, along which our orbit takes us throughout a year's time, made up of 12 "signs" through which all planets move.

Sign — one of the 12 equal parts of the Zodiac, each spanning 30 degrees of our sky and fixed to a certain part of the sky. The signs each symbolize different energy styles and influence planets that pass through their territory. Contrary to popular conflation, though they do bear the names of constellations, a sign and a constellation are not quite the same thing. Constellations, as I'm sure you know, are groupings of stars in the sky that are thought to represent images (I have always thought of them as cosmic dot-to-dot drawings). They do follow along the part of the sky where the planets travel — called the "ecliptic" — but they are not the same thing as the signs! (Who knew?!) While the constellations vary in size, a sign is a very particular 30° span of the sky that encircles us, each one being the same size. They are in the vicinity of the constellations for which they are named, but a sign is really just a span of space! Yet, it is thought to signify a particular energy, as has been witnessed for millenia. This circle of (mostly) animals has long been known as the Zodiac. A little zoo in the sky!

Becoming familiar with this arrangement and form of energies throughout the space around us lets us begin to understand our charts in the context of symbolic time. Every moment of time has its own quality. Some moments are hot, some are cool, some are frantic, some are still. Some bring the energies of the Lion, while others bring Scorpionic energies and ways of being.

Retrogrades, too, have their own flavor, which they add to our earthly experience. But, what is a retrograde? Let's go to the next section to find out more about them.

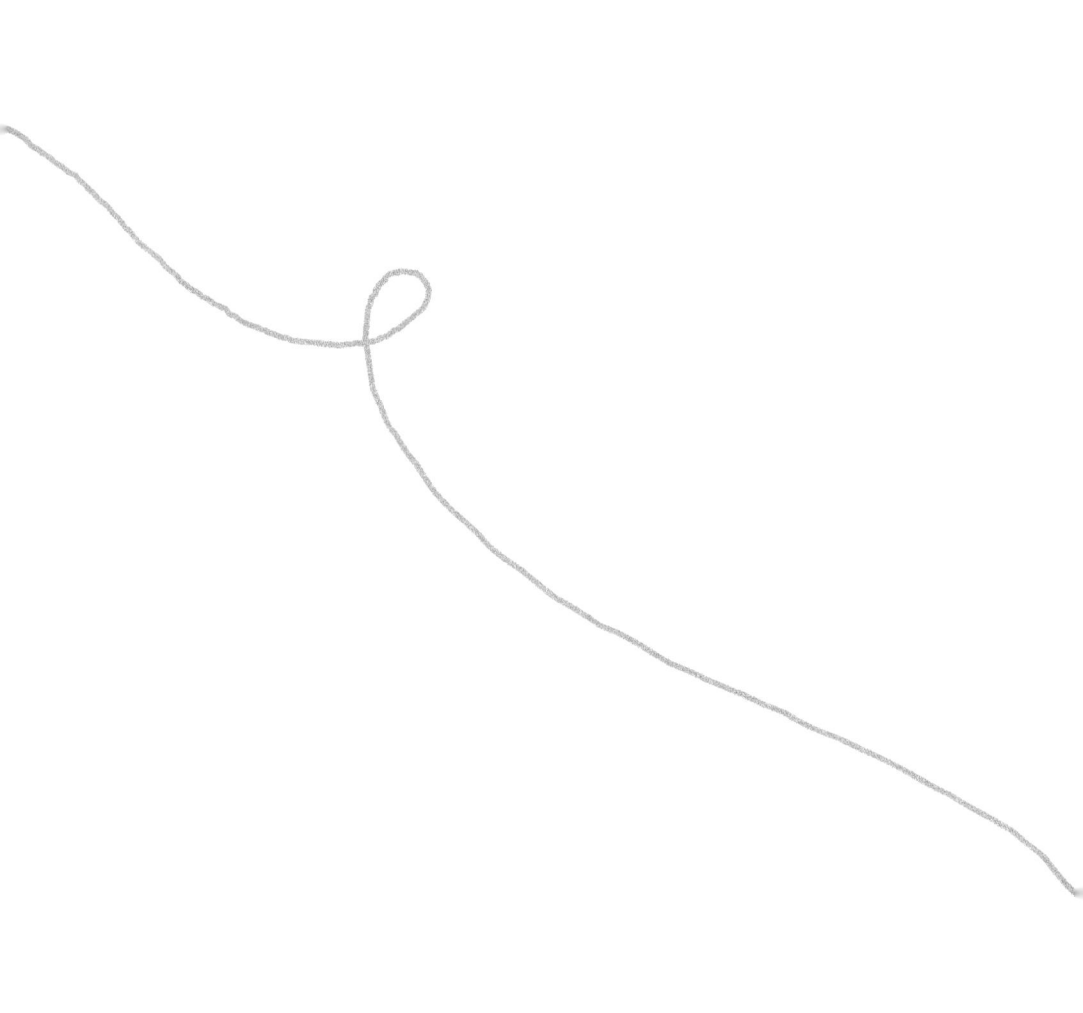

RETROGRADE
BASICS

"The way is not in the sky.
The way is in the heart."

~The Buddha

Retrograde Basics

Retrograde — when a planet appears to slow down, stop, and move backwards (a trick of perspective); a time when a planet's qualities and topics may be less straightforward.

You know those fairy tales in which the Heroine goes off of the main trail on her way to the Witch's house, only to meet a Magical Toad who offers the exact random bit of strange insight that our Brave Traveler will later need? That is how we can look at retrograde periods, believe it or not!

Retrogrades are oft thought to be "problem zones", but they actually present a unique opportunity to figure things out in a way that we never would if we simply rushed past these points in time.

Consider what would happen if the Brave Traveler never met the Magical Toad! They'd miss out on pertinent insight and may suffer for it. In light of this, it would behoove us to embrace the wisdom of "Retrograde Logic" for any retrograde period we encounter. When this logic is at play, things tend to move in a fashion that is contrary to the norm. It can feel like a time warp or a side-track — perhaps a dream? It may seem perturbing at the time, but can often be a very valuable detour in the overall scheme of things.

When you start to see all of the planets as weaving a magical-rainbow-helix-cord-of-time, you begin to understand that each thread — while making up part of the whole — has its own qualities and may even take on a directional variation, making eccentric passes as it meanders according to its own design.

These "floats" across the contemporary waffle-weave of time offer different opportunities than if they had remained rigidly congruent. Take Spanish lace, for example — an intricate form of lace, which I'm sure you can imagine, even if you've never seen it — without the deviant routes of particular parts of the pattern, we'd never get to enjoy the lovely end result!

This is, to some degree, how we can see periods known as retrogrades. They are deviations in the overall pattern, but not necessarily without purpose or a beauty all their own.

Retrogrades stretch time... but only for one topic at a time! That is, the whole weaving doesn't turn inside-out, but the pattern does indeed change for the planetary thread in question.

So: when there is a Mercury Retrograde, Mercury themes get stretched out over time and take a little circuitous route. When there is a Venus Retrograde, Venus themes get more depth and more interest than usual. When Mars turns retrograde, we really notice that Martian texture and direction. If you've been paying attention, you've certainly made note of such inclusions.

What you may not have thought of, though, is that this stretching of time offers us more opportunity to focus on the themes at hand and to work them out accordingly. Each in their own time! Of course, at times there are overlaps, which just means we have more in our travel baskets at those moments. And still, each side-track brings us potential allies and insights to enrich our journey.

So, try looking at each retrograde with curiosity about how it will stretch time for you. What will you learn then? What new tools or secrets will you glean from the frog in the wood? How can you take advantage of the extra time offered you?

It's not every day that we are given extra time — one of our most finite resources. What a gift!

So, it can be considered part of our task during any retrograde cycle to let go of our usual expectations in favor of a curiosity of mind that looks for this seemingly backwards logic that invariably drives us forward during these higgledy-piggledy times. Bringing awareness into the equation means you'll have a chance to play along with the quirky energy — which will hopefully keep you from being side-swiped or bull-dozed by it!

But what is a retrograde, really?

Retrograde describes a period of time during which a planet that is moving through space — up in our sky — appears to move backwards from our vantage point here on earth. The word retrograde comes from the Latin "retrogradi" meaning, literally, to step or walk backward — and many of us do indeed backpedal during retrograde experiences!

Planets don't actually move backwards, of course. They do appear to, but it is just a trick of the eye having to do with the complex celestial dance, of which we are but one moving part, wherein planets are going around the Sun and criss-crossing the sky, in reference to each other.

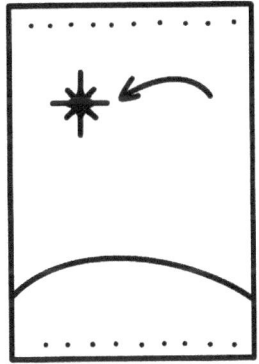 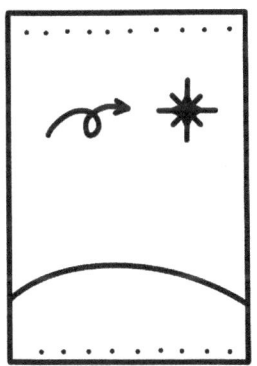 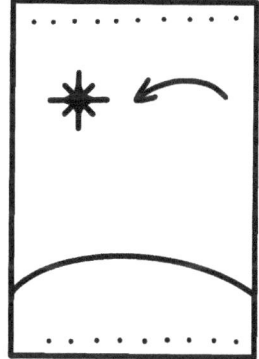

Regardless of the specifics of *how* this plays out from a Hubble-telescope point of view, over the centuries, attentive and well-trained skywatchers here on Earth have noticed that when planets appear to move backwards through our sky, the things (qualities, themes, and sometimes more literal manifestations) represented by those planets seem to come to the fore for reconsideration and renegotiation.

So, during a planetary retrograde cycle, as the planet appears to move backwards through our night sky — covering the same celestial territory three times over as it goes forward, then backward, and forward again — themes associated with the planet will be "up" for reexamination.

It is important to note that retrogrades often present in our experiential awareness as times of not-knowing. I have most often seen clients struggle with the topic at hand in a way that shows up as some form of opportunity presenting itself or some decision-point that comes up. In these cases, the retrograde period ends up being the time during which our brave explorer is unsure about what to do next; perhaps stepping back, back-pedaling, or re-considering things and, indeed, learning something they hadn't known before, which then informs their way forward.

It can be very uncomfortable for some to sit in such a period of not-knowing — particularly the longer periods offered by larger and more distant planets (like Saturn or Neptune) whose retrograde motions take much longer than the interior planets like Mercury, Venus, and Mars. When we are in a time of not-knowing, it can help to have a timeline suggesting how long it may last and to be able to recognize the themes at play. This is exactly why we are focusing on retrogrades in a purposeful way and making use of the tools at our disposal — the most potent of which are offered in these pages.

How to find a retrograde in your natal chart

Your personal natal chart is like a photograph or diagram of our solar system, as seen at the moment of your birth from the very place you were born. It is a map of the sky that never changes because it is a snapshot. It is the pattern of the planets at the moment of your birth, in diagram form.

As planets continue to move through our sky, each one reverberates with parts of our natal charts, astoundingly correlating to our personal experiences in very specific ways.

To find what part of your chart any retrograde is taking place in, you'll first need to know what your chart looks like. If you don't yet have a copy of your chart, you'll need to get one. I have made a "FREE Video Tutorial on How to Find your Chart" on my YouTube channel. You can find the address for it in Appendix E.

Then, once you know in which sign a retrograde is taking place, you simply find that sign in your chart to see what house (the little numbered "pie slices" of your chart) it is in. Each house signifies a different part of life.

Using the Keyword Lists found in Appendix A and B, along with your own chart, you will be able to create a personal keyword combination (your Magical Touchstone!) for guidance, and track what's happening for you during this retrograde cycle.

What retrogrades are and aren't good for . . .

What to avoid:

Generally, retrogrades are thought to be poor times to initiate anything having to do with the themes of the retrograde planet in question.

For example, with Mercury Retrogrades the common wisdom is to avoid starting new things having to do with Mercury's domain, which includes things like: communication, technology, meetings, logistics and other details. So, it is advisable to avoid things like: signing contracts, purchasing tech or appliances (including vehicles!), starting writing projects, or initiating new communication efforts.

If it is unavoidable that you do any of these things during a Mercury Retrograde, a common outcome is that some aspect of the effort won't be straightforward. There might be something that won't work and will have to be sent back, or a miscommunication affecting the ease and flow of a situation. It means that there could be complications to be worked through, that it may not be a one-and-done phenomenon.

If you can live with that, then don't even worry about the retrograde aspect! However, it can be really nice to avoid these complications.

Knowing about these potential "re-routes" heading into retrograde periods can allow us to go with the flow when these things do happen and avoid making a tricky situation worse!

For other planetary retrogrades, you'll want to apply this same general principle to the parts of life associated with that particular planet.

For instance, when either Venus or Mars are retrograde — both considered to be "personal planets" that are often associated with relationships — rekindling a relationship with an old flame may be ill-advised, as they tend to show up more as reminders of why it didn't work in the first place, rather than suddenly overcoming the problems of the past. Of course, it could also be that you need a refresher on the same lesson. In which case, you may find yourself diving right in! Whatever happens, having the retrograde setting as a lens through which you operate can help you contextualize your experience.

What to do:

While retrogrades are considered a poor time to start something new, they are thought to be suitable instead for finishing up old projects or working on things that need re-doing.

If you want or need to do something close to or during a retrograde period, one approach is to at least *start* a project before the retrograde has begun. That way, you can avoid starting it *during* the retrograde and will technically be finishing up something you'd previously begun. This seems to work for some.

Otherwise, if you absolutely must start or do something "forbidden" during a retrograde, be prepared to deal with additional trials and tribulations. It doesn't mean it won't work out, just that it might take more work to accomplish than it might have otherwise.

Often, the things that come up and need re-working during a retrograde are the result of an overwrought planetary function. For Mercury, this might be "speediness". Venus Retrogrades can bring up relational considerations, perhaps caused by an excess of softness; while Mars Retrogrades tend to bring up issues from past flames or anger that hasn't been dealt with, perhaps requiring a stronger separation or action to move the energy along. Watch for these themes during these various retrograde periods and see for yourself!

Another thing to keep in mind is that "Retrogrades gonna Retrograde". In other words, it will take the time it takes, so no sense in trying to hurry it along or wishing it wasn't happening. It happens! Knowing that it's happening can lend us grace in dealing with whatever comes up. Just as the breath goes in & out, the tide gets high & low, planets go retrograde & direct. It is part of the rhythm of life. Aligning ourselves with it can only help.

Finally, remember to keep the idea of "Retrograde Logic" in mind and consider looking at things inside-out, upside-down, and backwards for unexpected insight.

A quick recap

Don't:

- Don't panic! We're talking hiccups, not catastrophes!
- Don't expect things to go 100% smoothly; have grace.
- Don't start things ruled by the retrograde planet...if you can help it! If you can't help it, then *c'est la vie* and you gotta do what you gotta do; just be prepared for potential hiccups.

Do:

- Do remember "Retrograde Logic".
- Do start things *before* the retrograde is in play, or wait until after, if you can.
- Do go with the flow, and use grace when difficulties or detours arise.
- Do come up with a Magical Touchstone to accompany you on your journey.

VENUS

"Get out of your own way and
sparkle like crazy instead."

~Stacy London

Venus

Symbolically, Venus signifies a feminine energy that is beneficial to life; she is cool and moist and gentle. She loves beauty, harmony, relationship, and unification. She has an energy all her own that manifests differently depending on which sign she is in; which lens we are seeing her through.

To get to know her purest energy a little better before we take a tour through the signs, consider this list of Venusian qualities using VENUS as an anagram to discuss some of her more well-known significations.

V is for Value:
Value as in valuables, quality, and self-worth. Venus represents all of these things!

E is for Embody:
Embodiment is a feminine principle that Venus exemplifies. Whatever element she is in, she *is* that element (as opposed to Mars, for example, who might *do* that element).

N is for Nurture:
Nurturing is another feminine quality demonstrated by Venus at her best.

U is for Union:
Every planet has a tendency toward different effects. Just as Mars separates, Venus unifies.

S is for Savor:
Another feminine principle is taking your time; there is no hurry. Savor your pleasant sensory experiences. Venus would!

While she is most at home in the signs of Taurus and Libra — both of which she is said to "rule" — she has something to offer in every sign. As I said, each sign is a lens that translates her energy to us in its own way. There are many facets of Venus to explore, as seen through the qualities of each sign of the zodiac. As it turns out, we never do get to experience Venus free from one of these lenses, so it behooves us to learn a bit about each one, that we may have a fuller experience of our celestial friend, the feminine goddess of the skies.

Before we traverse the signs, it helps to know a bit about how the signs are described in astrological terms. Each sign is said to represent one of **four elements**: earth, water, fire, or air. They are also grouped into **three "modalities"** — their style of operating, if you will: Cardinal (initiating), Fixed (sustaining), or Mutable (dissolving). Where these groups of 3 and 4 overlap, we get 12 different combinations or expressions of energetic style.

One of the main practices of astrology becomes learning to combine symbolic expressions to discover their outcomes. It takes practice and life experience while considering such concepts to become truly adept, yet even using keywords can help to get anyone started. We will be using such keywords in our process a little later on to create our Magical Touchstones for the retrograde journey ahead.

Whether you are new to astrology or a seasoned professional, it may be fun and insightful for you to read through the following descriptions of potential manifestations of Venus through the signs. Though I consider myself a rather practiced astrologer, I still enjoy reading my colleagues' interpretations and continue to find or be reminded of little gems of thought, insight, or perception that serve my greater understanding. It's true that astrology is so complex that it is nearly impossible to hold the whole of it in our heart-minds at any one time.

In this spirit, I offer you the following descriptions, in hopes that they may serve your experience. Please note that these are exaggerated descriptions meant to elicit the vibe of each placement and are thus illustrative of potential manifestations of Venus through the signs. These descriptions are not meant to represent every person with such a placement. Each person's natal chart is too complex for that ever to work that way!

Please also note that, although I am referring to Venus as "her" to honor the feminine energy, it by no means is restricted to women, since we all have both masculine and feminine energies within us and all throughout the universe. As I suggested, these descriptions are meant to be caricatures to help bring the potential energy of different placements to life in your imagination. Read on for some impressions of Venus.

Venus Through the Signs

Aries
Element: fire
Modality: cardinal/initiating

Venus in Aries is "hot", assertive, and flirtatious. She connects through activity, initiates contact, and doesn't wait around for what she wants. She actively attracts, and a lot of her perceived beauty or charm is revealed in her face. She is independent and willful. She likes to be first, and does exactly as she pleases.

Taurus
Element: earth
Modality: fixed/sustaining

Venus in Taurus is rich and earthy. Focused on pleasure of all of the senses of the body, she appreciates the finer things in life like chocolate, quality bedsheets, and sturdy items made of natural materials. She delights in an abundance of plants, and loves gardens or forests. She is tactile, enjoying dynamic textiles and physical connection.

Gemini

Element: air

Modality: mutable/dissolving

Venus in Gemini is lighthearted and youthful. She sings and babbles poetry, or writes long eloquent ramblings in journals. She listens to the radio or the birds and does all kinds of hand work. She is curious and studies other people, delighting in connecting with them through ideas, imaginings, and talk-talk-talking.

Cancer

Element: water

Modality: cardinal/initiating

Venus in Cancer loves feeding people and otherwise taking care of them. She likes a clean home and cozy time, potentially surrounded by family or whomever offers her a feeling of comfort. She may be nostalgic or emotional, connecting through mutual care and emotional vulnerability.

Leo

Element: fire

Modality: fixed/sustaining

Venus in Leo attracts attention. She loves what she loves and enjoys being doted on and showered with gifts. She is playful, proud, and creative and does not shy away from opportunities to prove it! She laughs easily and prefers to be having fun.

Virgo

Element: earth

Modality: mutable/dissolving

Venus in Virgo pays attention to detail. She notices how things are made and appreciates craftsmanship and good design. She likes things orderly, is thrifty, and is very resourceful. She is constantly tending something and may always know how something could be better, yet can also be a very astute observer with discriminating taste.

Libra
Element: air
Modality: cardinal/initiating

Venus in Libra prefers company to being alone. Anything done in partnership is worth doing! She appreciates good manners, good hygiene, and beautiful design. She can be quite graceful and may seem to glide through a room. She can reason her way into — and out of — most anything. She is just and diplomatic.

Scorpio
Element: water
Modality: fixed/sustaining

Venus in Scorpio is seductive and loves a good mystery. She can be unconsciously secretive or simply not forthcoming. She may be interested in taboo subjects, whether that's sex or money or more esoteric and occult interests. She moves instinctively and trusts her gut more than any other input. With her, you are either in or you are out.

Sagittarius
Element: fire
Modality: mutable/dissolving

Venus in Sagittarius loves freedom and discovery. She is philosophical and interested in the big picture; what's over the next horizon. She is attracted to cultural expressions like poetry, music, food, and attire. Anything exotic is a curiosity. She is spontaneous and maybe sometimes bigger than her britches, but always fun to have around.

Capricorn

Element: earth
Modality: cardinal/initiating

Venus in Capricorn has high expectations about how things "should" be. She may enjoy more traditional tastes and palates. She is stately and seems to desire "the royal treatment" from others — even though she may be stingy with herself. She takes things a step at a time in a determined direction and always gets there eventually.

Aquarius

Element: air
Modality: fixed/sustaining

Venus in Aquarius can be a little quirky, yet charmingly lovable. People tend to be drawn to her clear ideas, even if — or especially if? — she is a little nonconformist. She is either not shy at all or incredibly shy, but just can't help but be noticed either way. She may have an avant-garde fashion sense, or her own way of doing things.

Pisces

Element: water
Modality: mutable/dissolving

Venus in Pisces is a sweet, sweet dreamer who may also be quite sensitive. She will be imaginatively creative, even if its only on the internal plane. She may dream vividly and have a strong intuition about people. It may take time to get to know her, but it is very rewarding to do so. She really cares a lot and may be spiritually attuned.

THE BEAUTIFUL
ASTROLOGY PROCESS

"When your soul awakens,
your destiny becomes urgent
with creativity."

~John O'Donohue

The Beautiful Astrology Process

The Beautiful Astrology Process for Retrogrades has three parts: Preparation, Engagement, and Reflection.

As part of Preparation, we become oriented to that which is at hand, including our natal charts, the planetary retrograde, and how the two interact. Part of the process of orientation includes putting all of the various pieces together with the use of keywords to create a Magical Touchstone. The Magical Touchstone could be a phrase, sentence, list, or symbolic image; but in all cases it will accompany us on our retrograde journey (we will begin that process soon).

The Engagement portion of the process involves "tracking" our experience — before, during, and after the retrograde — as the planet moves over the same part of the sky three times. Logging our experience helps us to see patterns and navigate the terrain with more wisdom and intention.

Lastly, the Reflection process at the end is super important to help us integrate our experience and everything we've learned; to carry forward what we'd like to remember from the experience and say a clear goodbye to the rest.

Now we begin the process of preparation. . .

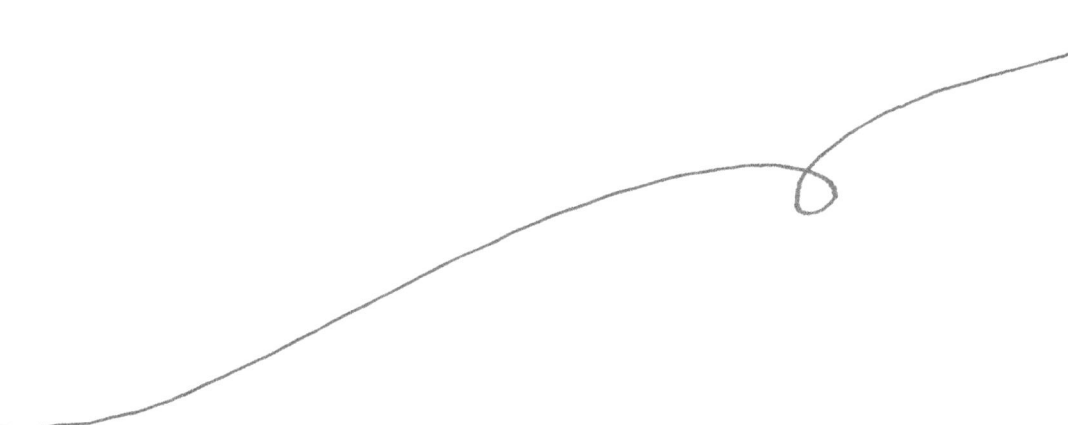

PREPARATION

"I arise in the morning torn between a desire to improve the world and a desire to enjoy the world. This makes it hard to plan the day."

~E. B. White

Preparation: Orientation through Keywords

While working with the symbolic qualities of the many parts that go together to form meaning using astrology, many find it useful to formulate coherent thoughtforms with the use of keywords to help make sense of the various energies at play.

Beginners and professionals alike can benefit from playing with keywords in this way, mixing their symbolic meanings together in a potpourri until a new, magical combination is found that resonates with the moment. This is partly why we refer to these keyword combinations as "Magical Touchstones". It is also because – though we use keywords to get started – sometimes what starts as a set of keywords morphs into a song or an image or a collage or a whole altar space!

In other words, we step into the process using keywords, but want to keep the outcome open to your own personal interpretation, to keep it most meaningful for you. So, please follow along and use the exercises to your advantage! But in the end, always give yourself permission to do what you know is right for you.

Another reason for the name is simply because this is how these magical little keyword phrases are experienced: they do seem to act as touchstones and retain a bit of magical mystery that helps to light the way – even when they don't encapsulate a retrograde experience as hoped or expected at the outset – they are always informative and worthy of our attention.

> **Magical Touchstone** – you will develop one of these for yourself to accompany you through this retrograde journey. It is a keyword-inspired creation of your own that you will be guided to form in this section as part of your preparation. It can help to focus your attention and can even help you navigate when you feel uncertain. It can take many forms in the end, but in the process presented here, it starts out as a set of keywords representing symbolic patterning.

These potent keyword combinations — Magical Touchstones — have proven to be invaluable companions for retrograde cycles in my planetary Retrograde Clubs. They're guideposts that we return to again and again throughout the retrograde cycle that provide both guidance and meaning.

Keywords for Retrograde Energy

The first keywords we will consider relate to the retrograde energy itself. Then, we will begin piecing keywords together in the guided sections that follow, bringing in the symbology of Venus, the sign/s she is traveling in, and even the house/s of your Natal Chart.

But, first things first: Retrograde Keywords!

Retrogrades are thought to be good times to do activities represented by RE- words, such as those listed below.

Here is a selection of RE-words for your consideration:

* Remember
* Restart
* Resist
* Rearrange
* Renew
* Redesign
* Reread

* Rewrite
* Renegotiate
* Reinstate
* Reassert
* Reword
* Reiterate
* Reimagine

Can you think of any other RE- words that might be important for you at this time? Write them here:

_____   _____

_____   _____

_____   _____

_____   _____

Can you remember when you took time to do one of these RE-words and it really paid off? Remind yourself here:

Venus Retrograde Themes

During any given Venus Retrograde cycle, we experience Venus Retrograde themes in the part of life indicated by the house (or houses) through which Venus will be traveling as she performs her retrograde back-and-forth dance. Though the sign (or signs) in which this happens add a flavor of their own, every Venus Retrograde has Venus in common.

So, when we ask "What are Venus Retrograde themes," what we're really asking is, "What are Venus themes?" That is, what themes are going to go on the loop-de-loop ride of the retrograde, bringing us new opportunities?

The retrograde part of the equation will be represented by one of the RE- words we considered in the last section. Below are some possible Venus themes that we may encounter during this Venus Retrograde cycle.

Venus themes may include:

♀ Relationship   ♀ Pleasure
♀ Connection   ♀ Fertility
♀ Care-taking   ♀ Money
♀ Beauty   ♀ Creativity

Can you think of any other keywords for Venus?
Write them here:

_____   _____

_____   _____

_____   _____

Now, let's explore the qualities of the sign/s that will be part and parcel of this Venus Retrograde experience.

Qualities of the Sign (or Signs)
of this Venus Retrograde

The qualities of the sign/s in question will show themselves through Venus Retrograde themes on this detour from what we normally experience in this part of our lives.

You already have an experience colored by this sign in some part of your life — according to the layout of your natal chart — so the quality itself is not necessarily new to you. What is new is the Venus Retrograde part of the story.

What qualities may get stirred up?

Using Appendix A, which lists keywords for all of the signs, write down as many of the keywords as you would like from the sign/s of the upcoming Venus Retrograde below (use Appendix C to find the sign/s for this Venus Retrograde):

The sign/s Venus will Retrograde through this cycle:

_____   _____

Keywords for the sign/s of this Venus Retrograde:

_____   _____

_____   _____

_____   _____

_____   _____

_____   _____

Magical Touchstone

Now you're ready to integrate the various themes that come together in a Venus Retrograde cycle by making a Magical Touchstone to act as your ally throughout your journey.

Please note that these touchstone phrases can sometimes play out as more of an attempt at wishful thinking than as a powerful touch point. This may be due to various factors, including both the possibility that the person creating the key phrase is wishing for their life to be different than it is, as well as the potential of the retrograde itself really shifting things. Though I have seen this happen in my planetary Retrograde Clubs, for the most part people have been spot-on in their phrase creation and have found their touchstones to be meaningful and useful in both subtle and profound ways. And, even when the experience differs from the hope of the keyword phrase, this is fertile information for the post-retrograde reflection process.

Creating your Magical Touchstone entails first playing around with the keywords until you find something intelligible that "sings" to you — that's how you'll know you've found a meaningful notion. You may need to rearrange the words or change their form. Try to allow your current truth to come through, even if it's not what you'd like.

Once you have created a Magical Touchstone, you can then use it as a lens through which you will observe your interior and exterior daily experience during this retrograde cycle. When things get tricky, you can come back to the phrase for comfort, awareness, orientation, direction, or whatever your particular phrase offers you during this time. Also, if you do note that it feels off, you may of course try again.

The lists you've already seen are here for you to play around with and come up with a Magical Touchstone that works for you. The process begins on the next page.

Create your Magical Touchstone

Record below the words for each category that seem the most pertinent for you at this time.

Write your most pertinent RE- word (from page 41) that is representative of the energy of a retrograde, here:

_____

And the Venus keyword (from page 43) that jumps out to you:

_____

Add a keyword for the sign or signs Venus is traveling through during this retrograde cycle (from page 44):

_____

Lastly, add a keyword for the house or houses in your chart that this sign is in (found in Appendix B), that will describe in what part of life this retrograde experience may show up for you:

_____

Here are some examples of Magical Touchstones people have used in the past for various planetary retrogrades:

- ◉ **Recalibrate my Money Skills**

- ◉ **Refresh Creativity — with Humor**

- ◉ **Listen for cues of Beauty redefining herself**

- ◉ **Renegotiate the boundaries between freedom and structure**

- ◉ **How can I help heal my heart?**

- ◉ **Refresh my self-reliance instinct**

Now, on the next page, put the words from the previous page together in a way that makes sense to you and record your Magical Touchstone for this retrograde cycle. There is extra space if you would like to use it for scratch paper or creative purposes. It's up to you!

MY MAGICAL
TOUCHSTONE

How to make the most of your Magical Touchstone

Now that you have a Magical Touchstone, what do you do with it? Well, it is up to you, but following is a discussion about its usefulness along with suggestions grown in the incubator of the Retrograde Clubs.

You may consider your Magical Touchstone to be an ally on the journey of this retrograde cycle. It could serve as a reminder of your intention, what this extended moment in your life is all about, how to navigate tricky terrain, or simply that you are indeed in the midst of a retrograde and may need to proceed in a way that differs from your normal mode of operation.

Others on the journey have found the following practices to be supportive:

1) Simply write down the phrase and place it where you will see it easily or carry it around with you for the duration of the retrograde cycle.

2) Make a playlist that epitomizes the sentiment of your phrase and listen to it regularly during the retrograde cycle.

3) Create a collage honoring your phrase and place it in a prominent place in your daily living space.

4) Use the phrase as a journal prompt to explore the ins and outs of what it could mean for you.

5) Use the phrase as a creative writing prompt to fashion a parable of your own journey as the Brave Traveler.

6) Create an Altar for this Venus Retrograde Cycle (see correspondence suggestions in Appendix D) and incorporate your own personal additions to exemplify your Magical Touchstone.

7) Choose an actual stone or gemstone to carry with you or place in a prominent location to be a physical reminder of your Magical Touchstone.

8) Dance it out! Or any other creative or embodiment process that makes sense to you.

Whether or not the creative suggestions appeal to you, it is important to keep the Magical Touchstone top of mind for your journey through the retrograde cycle.

For this reason, there is room to record it numerous times throughout the following pages, where you will record and track your lived experience. This gives you a chance to be reminded of your Magical Touchstone or to even revisit it and revise it (both very retrograde things to do!) should you find that it doesn't suit your experience once you have actually begun the journey through the retrograde cycle.

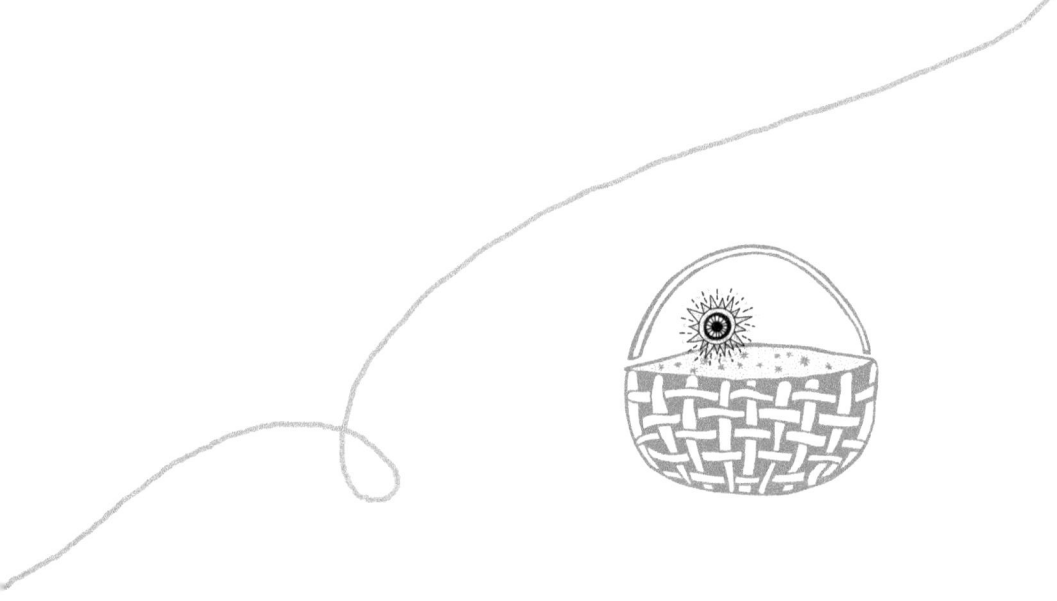

ENGAGEMENT: LOGGING YOUR LIVED EXPERIENCE

"The Soul is born in beauty
and feeds on beauty,
requires beauty for its life."

~ James Hillman

Engagement: Logging Your Lived Experience

Tracking your experience during the retrograde cycle helps raise your awareness as to your own patterns and pathways. It can help you navigate your own lifeway because you will have a clearer picture of what is actually happening for you — even when you are in the midst of what can be a time of not-knowing, as many retrogrades are.

The tracking pages include space for both external and internal factors in order to see if and how they relate. We also break up the tracking cycle into three periods: **Pre-Retrograde, Retrograde**, and **Post-Retrograde**.

Ideally, you would be able to begin tracking at the beginning of the cycle (during the Pre-Retrograde period), all the way through to "Reflections on this Venus Retrograde Cycle", which is best done after the Post-Retrograde period. But don't worry if you miss a portion of the Pre-Retrograde. It is not nearly as crucial as paying attention during the Retrograde itself — which helps you to navigate — and reflecting back Post-Retrograde, to collect what you can glean from your whole Venus Retrograde experience.

If you are beginning this process after the retrograde has already begun, just take some time now to reflect back on what has already happened during the Pre-Retrograde period (periods for each Venus Retrograde cycle through 2042 are listed in Appendix C).

Then, continue tracking as the retrograde progresses, through the Post-Retrograde period. Be sure to do the reflection exercises at the end of the workbook, where you will look back on your experience of the full retrograde cycle.

Pre-Retrograde Experience

My Magical Touchstone:

_____

This portion of the retrograde cycle is when topics may begin to emerge that will be focused on during the retrograde proper. It is worthwhile to pay attention and take even a few notes of your experience on the way in, so that when you get into the thick of it, you have your bearings.

Pre-Retrograde dates (see Appendix C):

_____

During this time, I am noticing the following . . .

Who I'm spending time with:

Activities I am engaged in:

Things occupying my mind:

Feelings I'm experiencing:

Questions I have:

Themes that are coming up:

Space for other notes:

Retrograde Experience

My Magical Touchstone:

_____

Here is where you'll log your experience for the retrograde portion of the journey. Remember that retrogrades can sometimes be periods of not-knowing. This does not mean that it is time to check out, however. Instead, it allows for time to check *in* in a more thoughtful way. It's like knowing that you have a whole chapter of a book for a character to learn a new secret that will help them solve the mystery in the next chapter. Remember: time gets "stretched" for the topic/s at hand. Take advantage of this opportunity by staying present with what is and recognizing the role it plays in your story. Record what you observe, think, and feel in these pages.

Retrograde dates (see Appendix C):

_____

During this time, I am noticing the following . . .

Who I'm spending time with:

Activities I am engaged in:

Things occupying my mind:

Feelings I'm experiencing:

Questions I have:

Themes that are sticking around from the Pre-Retrograde:

How they are developing:

Ways I can work with what is happening:

If I am experiencing not-knowing, what it is about:

Space for other notes:

Post-Retrograde Experience

My Magical Touchstone:

In this part of the journey, things may begin wrapping up. Or perhaps there is yet more to be done or more information to be gathered. Whatever was initiated in the Pre-Retrograde period that carried through and became prominent in the Retrograde period may now begin to resolve during this period until things are more or less wrapped up by the time this period ends and Venus moves along to another part of the sky.

Retrograde dates (see Appendix C):

During this time, I am noticing the following . . .

Who I'm spending time with:

Activities I am engaged in:

Things occupying my mind:

Feelings I'm experiencing:

Questions I have:

Themes that are sticking around from the Retrograde:

How they are developing:

Ways I can work with what is happening:

If I was experiencing not-knowing during the retrograde, some things that may be becoming clearer include:

Space for other notes:

What to do with your tracking notes

Now that you've paid attention to your journey and kept track of it in these pages, it's time to go back over your notes and reflect on what has happened. This can be an integral part of processing the retrograde cycle and is best done after the planet has gone direct or even cleared its shadow (so: after the dates you listed in the Post-Retrograde section). In this way, you are free of the energy at its topsy-turviest and may thus have a fairly clear — yet still fresh — perspective.

Before you begin your reflections in the next section, you may want to take a moment and be sure that you've jotted down everything of import that you want to consider before switching gears from experiential mode into reflection mode. Reflection is, by nature, meant to take you a step or two out of your direct experience so that you can observe yourself with a wider and perhaps unattached perspective; to help you see things more clearly. It is sometimes hard to see ourselves from inside of our lived experience. But, when we take a pause and look at our logged experience from the outside, it creates an opportunity to see ourselves a bit more clearly.

Also, now that you are out of the retrograde energy, the whole of the experience may come into focus in a way that it couldn't while it was happening. In the next section, take time to consider what the new you comprehends about your journey and its themes that you hadn't fully incorporated before the retrograde occurred.

REFLECTION: INTEGRATION & CLOSURE

"In Venus' world, beauty of form
and harmony of living heal and
uplift the human soul."

~Douglas Bloch & Demetra George

Reflection: Integration & Closure

Here is your opportunity to look back on the whole arc of your journey through the retrograde: from the Pre-Retrograde when the themes maybe first showed themselves as being "up" for reconsideration, through the Retrograde time of not-knowing or topsy-turviness, and into the Post-Retrograde period of tying up loose ends and resolutions of one form or another.

Now, you can reconsider the whole of the journey and explore what it means for you going forward.

My reflections on this retrograde journey

♀ What I've noticed

♀ What surprises me

♀ How I felt

♀ Where in my life this showed up

♀ Reflections on my Magical Touchstone

♀ What I'm leaving behind from this retrograde

♀ What I'm taking with me

Record your reflections on the pages that follow.

What I've noticed:

What surprises me:

How I felt:

Where in my life this showed up:

Reflections on my Magical Touchstone:

What I'm leaving behind from
this retrograde:

What I'm taking with me:

CLOSING THOUGHTS

"Venus likes us to banish the past before invoking the future."

~Caroline Casey

Closing Thoughts

ongratulations, weary traveler! You have made it through the entire planetary retrograde cycle. It is not always pretty, but it is a part of life, nonetheless. A part that recurs every year and a half, as it turns out. Next time Venus goes retrograde, though, it will be in a different sign and a different part of your chart — a whole new journey! Venus does cycle through the same few signs in 8 year increments, though, so it might be worth keeping these notes — or some portion of them — for future reference, in case similar themes arise at that time.

You can check Appendix C to see when the next Venus Retrograde cycle occurs (in about a year and a half) as well as the next time Venus will be retrograde in the same sign (usually about 8 years — until she shifts into another sign or set of signs as part of her long-term journey pattern).

In the meantime, you may wish to track Venus as she moves through the signs of the Zodiac — usually for just under a month at a time — until her next retrograde. You may use the keywords in this book to gain insight as to how the Venusian energies might show up in each sign. If you want to know what sign Venus is in, consider purchasing a quality astrology calendar, learning to look it up on an astrology website, or finding a quality app for quick reference on your phone (see Appendix E for recommendations). In this way, you can stay connected to the energy of Venus and get to know her better — and yourself — before the next retrograde comes around.

Regardless of how you spend your days, I wish you every blessing that you may receive on your journey! Thank you for engaging in this self-reflective experiential excursion. I hope you learned a lot and I hope to get to travel with you again in the future.

Blessings to you!

APPENDICES

"History, of the archetypal sort,
is a process in which
stories of infinite variety are
constantly being told."

~Shaun McNiff

Appendix A: Sign Keywords

I like to think of the signs as entire realms, of which we can only catch glimpses here and there. Each keyword is like a peek through a keyhole that lets us see a little bit more of the magical realm. Here are a few keywords to get you headed in the right direction, toward witnessing and understanding the wholeness of each of the signs.

Aries — Ram - Initiating, assertive, active, leading, spontaneous, anger, aggression, "hot-headed", pilgrim, warrior, head, beginner, new growth

Taurus — Bull - Sensuous, pleasant, slow, deliberate, pleasure, comfort, quality, value, beauty, throat, stubborn, easy-going, stability, luxury

Gemini — Twins - Inquisitive, curious, ingenious, ingenuitive, talkative, loquacious, scattered, changeable, arms & hands, of two minds

Cancer — Crab - Caring, cozy, nurturing, moody, powerful, emotional, tender, stomach, inner arms, breasts, home, cyclical, feeding/food, nesting, care-taking

Leo — Lion - Creative, expressive, regal, performer, light-bringer, love-light, heart, insisting, flamboyant, role-playing, playful, fun

Virgo — Woman - Organized, analytical, serving a higher purpose, tidy, orderly, studious, simplifier, resourceful, thrifty, nutrition, stomach & digestion, tending, efficient, sovereign, details, rules, purity, patterns, improvement

Libra — Scales - Balance, justice, harmony, social, partnership, my way or the highway, kidneys, beauty, diplomatic, design

Scorpio — Scorpion - Sacred, taboo, secret, power, depth, truth, underworld, sex organs, elimination, intense, reserved

Sagittarius — Archer - Seek, expand, explore, freedom, travel, beliefs, fun-loving, adventure, religious/philosophical, run/walk/dance, movement, dogs and horses, advocacy, righteousness, enthusiasm, hips, buttocks and thighs

Capricorn — Sea Goat - Responsible, planner, time-conscious, big picture, uber-practical, success-oriented, boss, knees, teeth, bones, driven

Aquarius — Water Bearer - Unique, weird, humanitarian, inventive, visionary, detached, avant-garde, belonging, big ideas, shins and ankles, circulation, eccentric

Pisces — Two Fishes - Compassion, oneness, fanciful, flighty, shy, boundary-less, dreamy, sensitive, idealist, imagination, symbolism, music, film, spiritual, escapist, introspective, permeability, blending, dreamy eyes, feet, aura

Appendix B: House Keywords

Here are some commonly accepted meanings of the houses to get you started.

First — Identity, the body, personality, projection, what people first notice, how you are perceived

Second — Possessions, value, worth, your money, earning

Third — Communication, learning, local travel, errands, vehicles, community, siblings, neighbors, skills

Fourth — Home, roots, ancestors, DNA, inherited culture, parent

Fifth — Creativity, fun, blessings, projects, children, fertility

Sixth — Health, daily tasks, job, routine, pets

Seventh — Relationship, partnership, clients, contracts, "known enemies"

Eighth — Shared resources, sex/death/taxes, collective, investment, psychic/ancestral energies & experiences

Ninth — Travel, higher education, religion, philosophy, divination, publishing, astrology

Tenth — Career, public role, position in greater world, parent

Eleventh — Friend-groups, networking, hopes and dreams

Twelfth — Solitude, isolation, spirituality, subconscious, one's "shadow", sleep, unknown enemies, hidden

Appendix C: Retrograde Dates

Venus Retrograde Cycles from 2023-2042

Note: all times listed in Universal Time; dates for your location may be "off" by one day.

2023   Leo
Pre-Retrograde: Jun 19-Jul 21
Retrograde: Jul 22-Sep 3
Post-Retrograde: Sep 4-Oct 7

2025   Pisces & Aries
Pre-Retrograde: Feb 23-Mar 1
Retrograde: Mar 2-Apr 12
Post-Retrograde: Apr 13-May 15

2026   Libra & Scorpio
Pre-Retrograde: Aug 31-Oct 1
Retrograde: Oct 2-Nov 13
Post-Retrograde: Nov 14-Dec 15

2028   Gemini
Pre-Retrograde: Apr 7-May 9
Retrograde: May 10-Jun 22
Post-Retrograde: June 23-Jul 26

2029-2030   Capricorn
Pre-Retrograde: Nov 15-Dec 15
Retrograde: December 16-Jan 25
Post-Retrograde: Jan 26-Feb 28

2031   Leo
Pre-Retrograde: Jun 17-Jul 19
Retrograde: Jul 20-Sep 1
Post-Retrograde: Sep 2-Oct 5

2033 Pisces & Aries
Pre-Retrograde: Jan 26-Feb 26
Retrograde: Feb 27-Apr 9
Post-Retrograde: Apr 10-May 13

2034 Libra & Scorpio
Pre-Retrograde: Aug 29-Sep 29
Retrograde: Sep 30-Nov 10
Post-Retrograde: Nov 11-Dec 13

2036 Gemini
Pre-Retrograde: Apr 5-May 7
Retrograde: May 8-Jun 19
Post-Retrograde: Jun 20-Jul 24

2037-2038   Capricorn
Pre-Retrograde: Nov 11-Dec 13
Retrograde: Dec 14-Jan 22
Post-Retrograde: Jan 23-Feb 23

2039 Leo
Pre-Retrograde: Jun 14-Jul 16
Retrograde: Jul 17-Aug 28
Post-Retrograde: Aug 29-Oct 12

2041 Pisces & Aries
Pre-Retrograde: Jan 24-Feb 23
Retrograde: Feb 24 - Apr 6
Post-Retrograde: Apr 7-May 11

2042 Libra & Scorpio
Pre-Retrograde: Aug 26-Sep 26
Retrograde: Sep 27 - Nov 7
Post-Retrograde: Nov 8-Dec 12

Appendix D: Correspondences

Offered here are suggestions for correspondences to symbolize the energies at play for Venus and the signs of the Zodiac for you to use in altar building or however you see fit (collage creation, fashion expressions, etc.). Feel free to use these as a starting place and follow your intuition or other sources for personalizing your symbolic connection to the energies at play during this Venus Retrograde cycle.

Venus: Female figures, flowers (especially rose or jasmine), jewelry, copper, rose quartz, olives, fruits, white, ocean creatures or shells, pretty bows or ribbon, hearts, money, peace symbols, artist's palette, anything representing beauty, harmony, artistry, marriage, unity, or refinement. The Empress tarot card.

Aries: Ram, fire, red, yellow, the head, anything representing leadership, movement, assertiveness, or action. The Emperor tarot card.

Taurus: Bull, earth, green, pink, the five senses, the neck or throat, hand-made items, plants or moss, delectable delicacies, anything representing steady work, handicrafts, generosity, or long-lasting quality. The Hierophant tarot card.

Gemini: Twins, air, rainbow, hands, communication tools (radio, reading, writing, speaking, listening, phone, computer, etc.), anything representing communication, learning, logic, information, or inquisitiveness. The Lovers tarot card.

Cancer: Crab, water, blue, shells, Moon, breasts, arms, pearl, nest, representations of home, family, nurturing, or comfort. The Chariot tarot card.

Leo: Lion, other big cats, fire, hot pink, orange, gold, Sun, heart, chest, back, spine, sunstone, crowns or other symbols of royalty or pride. Strength tarot card.

Virgo: Maiden, earth, greens and browns, stomach, digestive tract, winged woman, anything representing studiousness, service, tending, or honesty. The Hermit tarot card.

Libra: Scales, air, kidneys, other tools of measurement, anything representing civility, sound judgement, diplomacy, or quality of life. Judgement tarot card.

Scorpio: Scorpion, water, black, maroon, dark red, sex organs, blood, bones, anything representing mystery, depth, death, or the occult. Death tarot card.

Sagittarius: Archer, centaur, horse, dog, fire, dark red, purple, buttocks, thighs, legs, walking, running, travel, shiny/shimmery objects, arrows/arrow-heads, pen, books, anything representing adventure, expansion, enthusiasm. Temperance tarot card.

Capricorn: Sea Goat, goat, fish, mountain, earth, dark brown, knees, skeletal structure, anything representing hard work, time, practicality, or determination. The Devil tarot card.

Aquarius: Water Bearer, vase, pitcher, air, shins, ankles, anything representing individuality, weirdness, or the future. The Star tarot card.

Pisces: Fishes, mermaids, whales, water, ocean creatures, ocean colors (purples, teals, shimmery blues), moonstone, shells, feet, anything representing compassion, spirituality, or oneness. The Moon tarot card.

Appendix E: Resources

Following are some recommendations for media that I have found useful or meaningful in tracking my own astrology.

Media Recommendations

The American Ephemeris — Learning to read an ephemeris is an essential skill for any astrology student. It is up to each student whether to choose an ephemeris set for Noon or one set for Midnight (follow your gut or discuss with qualified astrologers). I would start with The American Ephemeris for the 21st Century 2000-2050 (mine is set at Noon) so you can keep up with what is happening now. Mine is by Neil F. Michelsen and Rique Pottenger. Recommended for intermediate students through professional level astrologers.

Astro Gold app — This is a paid app that allows you to do a lot of cool things with charts, not the least of which is looking up the chart of the moment to see what the planets are doing right now (or any time, really — within reason, at least). You can also watch time move forward or backward in this app, which is one of the best features about it, I'd say. Search for it wherever you buy apps. Recommended for intermediate level students through professionals.

AstroDienst website ("astro.com") — A comprehensive astrology website made by astrologers for astrologers with a lot of information, articles, and different ways to access astrological information. You may register with them to create a profile and save up to 100 different charts for free while you are learning (you can save many more with a very reasonably priced subscription). Recommended for beginners through professionals. Learn more at astro.com

> Find my video *How to Find Your Natal Chart Online* for assistance navigating astro.com at this address: https://youtube.com/@beautifulastrologymelanie

The Astrology Podcast — A quality production that takes astrology seriously as an academic pursuit. Offers annual and monthly forecasts and covers topics ranging from beginner to professional level, including the basics of astrology, historical context and findings, as well as topics of current interest in the broader astrological community. Find it online at theastrologypodcast.com or wherever you find your podcasts. Recommended for all levels interested in an academic approach.

Dreamfruit Almanac — A lunar-based planner and interactive almanac for earthlings by Elizabeth Russell. Dreamfruit tells the story of the year, New Moon by New Moon, through rich symbolism gleaned from the astrology of the time, the wisdom of the "Sabian symbols", and Elizabeth's own insightful thematic weaving. Recommended for all levels of astrological experience — including *none*! — since it focuses on personal experience and the timely themes that are offered in the text for each moon cycle (approximately each month). Learn more at her website: www.Dreamfruit.world

Honeycomb Almanac — An astrological almanac that includes daily astrological data for the world in general as well as specific to your very own chart! Highly recommended for intermediate students through professional astrologers. No interpretations are offered, but there is so much (personalized) information; a true treasure trove for those who are adept at reading and understanding the language of astrology. Made by two really neat humans. Learn more at honeycomb.co

The landscape within — By this, I mean your own internal "terrain" and that which takes place where no one can see. One recommendation I have for anyone wanting to use astrology to their benefit is to keep a journal (make sure to write the DATE)! I confess that I cycle in and out of this, myself, but every time I want to look back and see what was happening under some transit that might relate to what's happening now, I *wish* that I had been better about keeping a journal. So: keep a journal! If not for yourself, then for your astrologer! You'll both be glad you did.

The Mountain Astrologer magazine — A print and digital magazine that has been around for decades, informing and featuring astrology enthusiasts of all levels. Subscribe to receive current issues and order past issues all the way back to 1997! Learn more at mountainastrologer.com

NORWAC — The Northwest Astrology Conference, held in Tukwila, Washington each Memorial Day Weekend, offers the opportunity to connect with astrologers of all levels while also attending a variety of lectures and gaining access to the biggest in-person (pop-up) collection of astrology books for sale in the country — if not the world — by Astrology et al Bookstore. Shop at astrologyetal.com, where you can also purchase recordings of lectures from past NORWACs. Recommended for all levels of astrology enthusiasts. Learn more at norwac.net

The sky above — By this, I mean the actual sky above. Remember that astrology has developed over millennia by careful skywatchers. Once you tune into the planets — let alone the cycles of the Moon — you won't believe that you never noticed them before! They are so bright and beautiful. There are so many astronomy and star-gazing websites and apps now, that I'm sure you will have no trouble finding ways to identify the planets. It can be wonderful to gaze upon them and see how it feels to let them gaze upon you. Perhaps you will even converse. Or sing! This is a highly recommended activity for all levels. You don't have to go any further than your own backyard—or driveway, window, balcony, or roof— whatever you have access to. Go see!

Time Passages app — A free app (with paid options) that allows you to see what sign each planet is in today — and read a generic interpretation for it. You may also save your natal chart AND get a daily horoscope, in the style of interpretations for each planetary placement and active "transit" to your chart. Recommended for beginner to intermediate students.

Your local Astrological Association — If you can find one! Even if there is not one in your town, there may be one nearby that you could travel to for monthly lectures or events. There are also national and international associations that meet online, if you are interested. I'm sure you can find them with a simple online search. Meeting up with other astrologers can feel like coming home...or landing on another planet (in the best way)! If you can't find a group that suits you, perhaps you can start one.

If you have enjoyed this guidebook, keep an eye out for its companions, which follow the same process for Mars Retrogrades (every two and a half years) for Mars themes — such as anger, passion, action — and Mercury Retrogrades (three or four times each year — there is just one book for the whole year) for Mercury themes such as communication, technology, and logistics.

Illustrations provided by Leah Rose, a young artist from Portland Oregon, who is confused about life but loves to make art while traveling the world.

Diagrams on pages 10, 11, and 19 by E. Edwards, a creative youth living in Washington state.

Look for more **Beautiful Astrology** titles at

https://elizabethrussell.space/earth-dragon-press/

EARTH
DRAGON
PRESS

Drawing on over 20 years of facilitating and teaching experience, Melanie Gurley offers practical guidance to help you deepen your understanding of your own rhythms and potentials.

Through exploration of the natal chart and tracking transits as they happen, you'll begin to recognize your life's patterns and find deeper meaning while contextualizing your experience.

Earth Dragon Press
exists to awaken the deep imagination as a
vibrant portal to the voice of
Earth & Cosmos. Our books inspire your
creative nature, with the purpose of
brightening the Earthling path.

Discover these and future titles at

https://elizabethrussell.space/earth-dragon-press/

EARTH
DRAGON
PRESS